# GET CREATIVE

# GET CREATIVE

Over 60 exercises, activities
and prompts to stimulate
your imagination

## LISA DYER

SIRIUS

**SIRIUS**

This edition published in 2018 by Sirius Publishing, a division of
Arcturus Publishing Limited,
26/27 Bickels Yard, 151–153 Bermondsey Street,
London SE1 3HA

ISBN: 978-1-78888-665-9
AD006588UK

Printed in China

# CONTENTS

# INTRODUCTION: HOW TO USE THIS BOOK

**This creativity book** is not concerned with goals or achievements in a linear way – it is a workbook to help you free up your mind and unchain your potential, unbridle your passions, release yourself from habitual thinking, and give you tools to be more organic and creative in your work and home life, as well as get in touch with your inner artist, in whatever form that takes. As a result you can skip around the book, dipping into it at any point. The exercises are designed to get your creative unconscious mind firing, to help you think a little differently and have some fun.

Organized thematically, the chapters will take you through a specific approach to creativity. The first chapter will help you find the time and head space to get started – so often the hardest hurdle to overcome. Subsequent chapters focus on **exploring** your **emotions** and **senses**, **challenging** your **perspectives** and **problem solving**, **word games**, and **art and design activities**. Throughout, a range of disciplines is employed. These include simple drawing, journalling, mindfulness activities and techniques to stimulate your creativity and help you think outside the box.  Treat every entry as a new experience and use it as a springboard to take you down other avenues, exploring disciplines and ideas you may never have considered before.

# CHAPTER 1

## MAKE SPACE FOR CREATIVITY

Creativity isn't something we can always call on at will, much though we would like to do so, but we can take steps to put ourselves in a receptive frame of mind and in an environment that is conducive to inspiration and invention. Through decluttering, time management and mindfulness techniques, you will discover ways to make your physical workspace more stimulating, as well as methods to give you the head space you need for new ideas to flourish.

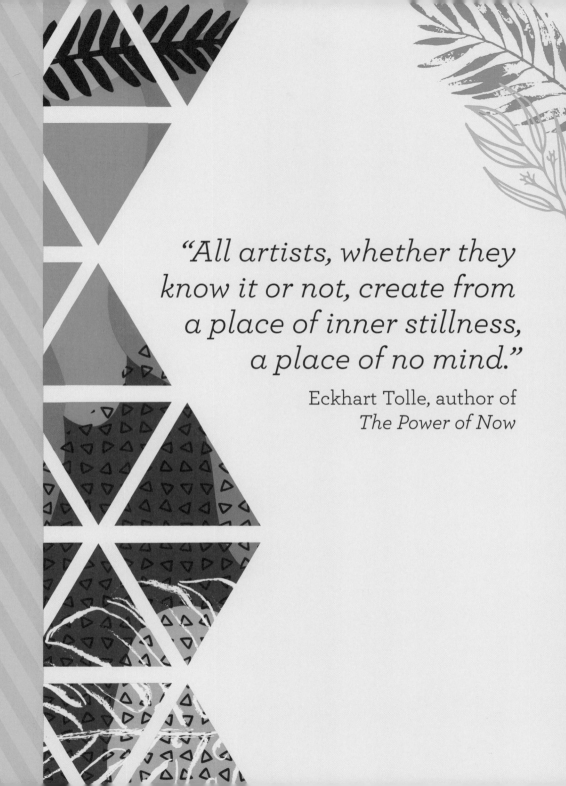

"All artists, whether they know it or not, create from a place of inner stillness, a place of no mind."

Eckhart Tolle, author of *The Power of Now*

# Create a Zen Space

Spend time creating a zen-like area that is just yours. It can be your office, cubicle or desk, a home work or craft area, your bedroom or even a favourite armchair in the corner of your living room. This will be your go-to place for inviting in imagination, a place where you can daydream, write, work or just retreat in order to think about ideas.

*Here are a few ways to super-charge this creative space:*

○ Completely clear clutter and anything that does not enhance your creative energy.

○ Decorate the area with visual "clues" that help you feel receptive, such as a colour that inspires or calms you.

○ Keep it simple: airy, clean and bright. Dust, wipe down and organize your space regularly.

○ Hide the clock, along with any non-essential electronic equipment.

○ Keep supplies stored away but within easy reach.

○ Buy items that encourage you to use them and that feel nice to use, such as colourful markers or pens, beautiful stationery or notebooks.

○ Add inspiration: a motivational quote on the wall, a plant, a moodboard.

○ Make sure the furniture is comfortable and at the right height for you.

# Mindfully Meditate into Your Flow State

This guided breathing exercise will help to kickstart your creativity and get ideas flowing by eliminating distractions and scattered thoughts. It will give you the head space for creativity and encourage the all-important "flow state" – when you are fully engaged and harmoniously "in the zone".

Sit comfortably in a chair and close your eyes.

Take 10 slow connected breaths. As you begin to relax, visualize yourself in a wooden boat on a lake; hear the waves lapping and feel the gentle motion of the boat. You feel the warm sun and breeze; everything is peaceful and tranquil.

Now paddle slowly into the centre of the lake, breath in as you pull the oars towards you; breathe out as you push them away. The rhythm of the oars is slow, steady. This is your flow, your rhythm. You are at one with the boat and its uninterrupted glide through the water. The shore becomes more distant behind you as you grow closer to an island ahead of you.

Continue breathing and paddling. When you reach the shore, step out onto the dock and tie up the boat.

# Breathwork

The word inspiration, with its overtones of divine guidance, has its roots in *inspirare*, the Latin for "breathe into", and this breath meditation will help calm and clarify your thoughts, increase awareness and focus, and create a space for inspiration. The best thing about this exercise is that it can be done anywhere and takes so little time but delivers a big impact.

1 Close your eyes and breathe in through your nose for a count of four, feeling your lungs fill and your belly expand.

2 Hold for a count of four, feeling your breath in your throat.

3 Exhale through your mouth for a count of six.

4 If your mind strays, return to the focus on your breath. Repeat six times.

# Draw Your Breath

The way, style and pace of your breath can have a dramatic impact on your mind and body. Deep breathing ensures oxygen is carried throughout your body, energizing all the cells and muscles. Inhales are energizing and uplifting; exhales aid relaxation and grounding.

○ Place a pen or marker on a blank sheet of paper. Close your eyes and draw your breath in a continuous line without lifting the pen. You will draw peaks and troughs as you breath in and out.

○ Now open your eyes and look at your drawing.

○ What do you notice? Is your breath quick and rapid, or slow and deep? Is it regular or erratic? Try slowing your breath down and draw again. Now try to extend your exhale to twice your inhale.

> *"The creative is the place where no one else has ever been. You have to leave the city of your comfort and go into the wilderness of your intuition. What you'll discover will be wonderful. What you'll discover is yourself."*
>
> Alan Alda, actor

# Find Your Quiet Place

Sometimes it's difficult to tune out the world so you can come up with an idea, and maybe it's physically impossible because you are in a busy environment both at work and at home. So create your own quiet place to go to in your head, which will be there whenever you need it.

❍ Find a comfortable place to sit and be still. Close your eyes. If there's lots of outside noise, put in earplugs or headphones. Make sure your back is straight and supported by your chair.

❍ Imagine your favourite quiet place. What does it look like? What sounds do you hear? You could be alone on the beach with just the pounding waves and seagulls in the background. Fill in as much detail as you can. You can come back here as often as you like, whenever you need some space of your own.

# Go Slow

Our daily lives are usually filled with one task after another, and we're encouraged to get as much done as fast as we can, as if there were a prize at the end for accomplishing the most in one day. But creativity and ideas can't flourish in a crowded space! Performing your day-to-day tasks in a slow, mindful way reminds you that you don't need to rush through life, that you are in control of the pace you are setting, and you can make a decision to be in the present.

Try taking a bus, or if you have to drive, move into the slow lane and enjoy the trip rather than focus on the destination!

What did you see on your trip?

Or walk at half your normal speed and notice your surroundings and other people – look around you and upwards. You'll be sure to see something you haven't noticed before, which can stimulate you in a creative way, or perhaps make you appreciate things others have created.

What did you notice on your walk?

Eat your meals slowly, taking time to be mindful of each bite, noticing the flavour and texture of the food. Concentrate on what you are eating, where the food came from, how it got to your table and who helped it on its way.

Describe your meal in tactile words, such as spicy, bitter, sharp, smooth, firm, zesty, aromatic.

# Take a Nature Break

When you have a creative block, your head is spinning, or you just can't focus, go outside where you can breathe in fresh air, feel the sun and connect with planet you live on. The combination of removing yourself from negative energy and taking physical exercise is a really powerful tool to stimulate creativity and resolve problems.

If there are practical reasons why you can't go to a nearby park or take a short walk, have a virtual forest bath instead. *Shinrin-yoku* is the act of slowly and mindfully walking through a natural wooded area in your imagination, and is reputed to deliver calming, rejuvenating and restoring benefits.

Sit in your chair, close your eyes, and take a few deep breaths. Allow your body to relax and feel your breath deepen and slow.

You are now in a forest with tall trees all around you and you can see the patterns they make against the blue sky. Sunlight dapples through the leaves, angling light across the path in front of you. Walking slowly, you notice the forest floor carpeted with fern and wildflowers – you can smell their delicate fragrance. You can hear the wind rustling in the trees and the birds chirping, and a trickling of water from a stream. The forest is alive and you are one with it. Spend some time visualizing your surroundings before opening your eyes.

# Declutter Your Desk

A very messy desk is a visual image of chaos – it contributes to any chaos you are feeling and makes a workload feel more insurmountable. To ensure your visual image of your surroundings is clean, clear and ordered, and a space in which you can come up with your best ideas, get busy with organizing your desk space. You deserve to have a clear, ordered start to each day.

○ Make piles or fill out the lists opposite: List One for things you use every day and need to hand – essential items and tools for creating; List Two for more seldom-used items, such as research materials or logbooks; List Three for items you won't need in the foreseeable future or no longer need; List Four for items you like but that serve no purpose.

○ Place all the items in List One in drawers close to you. Place all the items in List Two on shelves or in harder-to-reach storage areas. Discard or give away all items in List Three. All the items in List Four are potential inspirational boosters and motivators – display these on a noticeboard or on your desk. Allocate time to do this every week.

List One:

List Two:

List Three:

List Four:

# Your Workspace Motto

We all spend lots of time at a computer, yet we often treat our desk environment like a necessary evil. Despite the fact that some companies make creativity a key goal of their office design, many of us are trying to create in an austere environment. Creativity breeds creativity, so start accessorizing your office by making a motivational postcard.

○ Design your cut-out-and-keep postcard opposite, for sticking to your computer or on a desk wall or shelf. You could choose a positive quote or affirmation, such as "Today Is a Good Day", "Remember to Breathe" or "Think Outside the Box". Alternatively draw or cut out an image that inspires and motivates you. Use colourful marker pens to embellish the postcard and stick it to your computer, shelf or desk. Use it as a prompt when you need to recharge or stimulate.

# CHAPTER 2

## AWAKEN YOUR SENSES

The exercises on the following pages will help you express your feelings and tap into the deep, rich well of your emotions and senses. Although feeling happy, upbeat or elated is associated with increased creativity, it's building connections between things – sometimes disparate, unrelated things – that creates the most energy and innovation. Here you will find out how to use your emotions and your five senses in combination and isolation to jumpstart your creative process.

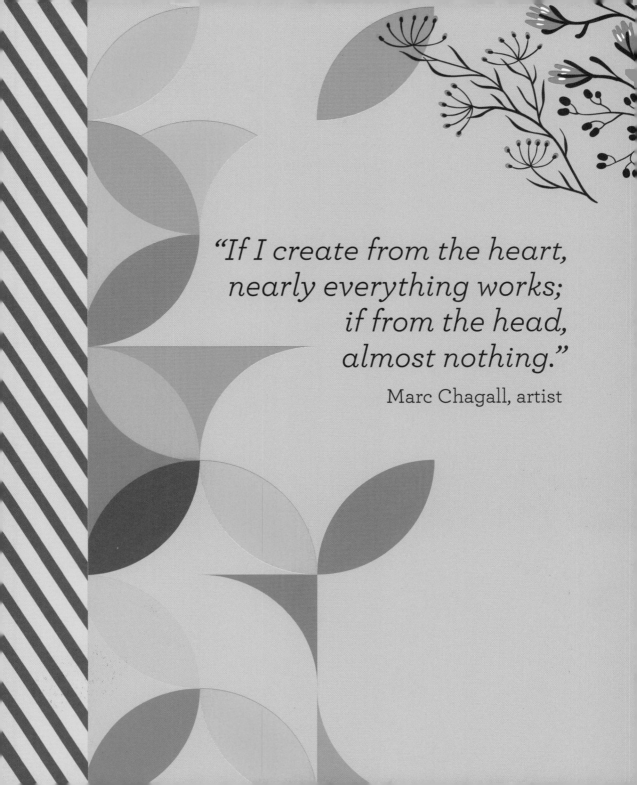

*"If I create from the heart,
nearly everything works;
if from the head,
almost nothing."*

Marc Chagall, artist

# Make a Sense Memory

This exercise is used by actors in order to get in touch with an imaginary backstory of a character and make it become real to them and the audience. They then recall the memory to tune into the "truth" and emotions of their character. Here you will be doing it with an authentic memory of your own.

Draw a place that you remember from your childhood – a holiday spot, a room in your childhood home, a schoolyard, an outdoor space. What did it look like? How did it feel? What did it smell like? Was it hot or cold and how hot or cold was it? Was it snowing or raining or did you feel the sun beating down on you and the grass. What sounds could you hear – bees buzzing or birdsong in the air? Use your five senses to describe all the visual details and physical sensations of the place.

# Take a Minute

Getting in touch with the breadth and depth of your emotions on a daily basis can make it easier to tap into your feelings at times when you need to be creative. Reflect on your inner thoughts and acknowledge them.

Stop right now and ask yourself how you are feeling emotionally: are you elated, happy, bored, angry? Circle 10 words below that describe how you are feeling right now, or add your own. Try to do this every day.

| | | |
|---|---|---|
| afraid | bored | conflicted |
| angry | calm | confused |
| annoyed | caring | content |
| apathetic | compassionate | creative |
| apprehensive | competitive | defeated |
| balanced | concerned | defensive |

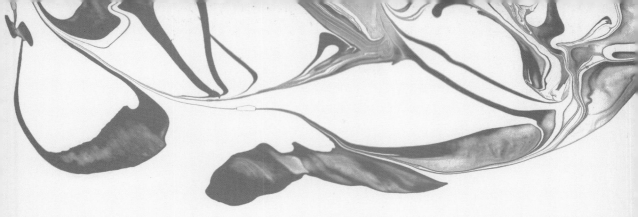

depressed

disappointed

disgusted

distracted

embarrassed

enthusiastic

envious

excited

exhausted

frustrated

fulfilled

grateful

grounded

grumpy

guilty

happy

heartbroken

hopeful

hurt

indifferent

insecure

joyful

kind

lazy

lonely

loving

nervous

neutral

overwhelmed

proud

relaxed

relieved

resentful

restless

sensitive

stressed

strong

suspicious

thankful

torn

trusting

vulnerable

worried

*"Ideas are like fish. If you want to catch little fish, you can stay in the shallow water. But if you want to catch the big fish, you've got to go deeper. Down deep, the fish are more powerful and more pure. They're huge and abstract. And they're very beautiful."*

David Lynch, movie director

○ Draw your "ideas fish" here! Make them as crazy and otherworldly as you like.

# Sensory Chamber

We live in a visual world and often over-rely on our sense of sight before all others. This exercise will help you tap into some of your other senses, such as hearing, smell and touch, to redress the balance.

Sit in a comfortable position – you can be in a room or outside in a park, anywhere you like. Now close your eyes.

What do you hear? What is the loudest thing you hear? What is the softest? What can you smell? Isolate each odour and name it.

## Music Appreciation

Music is mood altering and can aid relaxation. This exercise will help you emotionally connect to music and listen to it in an interactive, rather than passive, way.

Play a piece of music without lyrics – it could be any style, such as jazz, classical or techno. Play it one time through, then play it again from the beginning, really listening, and write down what you see in your mind's eye: it may be particular images, as in an unfolding story; it may be feelings, sensations or colours.

Concentrate on the tone, mood and feel of the music – does it feel happy, sad, frenetic, mournful?

Imagine the music as a scene – what is the dominant colour, what action is taking place?

Is the sound as timid as a mouse, as bold as a marching band, smooth like water, crackling like fireworks? Be as descriptive as you can.

## Textures and Patterns

Our sense of touch tells us so much about the world we interact with – the size and shape of things and how we can use them; for example, if something is wet and slippery, dense and heavy, sharp or malleable.

Draw, photograph or cut out from a magazine three images showing texture. In nature these might be the rough bark on a tree, pebbles on a beach, or a crisp, veined fallen leaf. Or it could be something manufactured, such as a brick wall, a wooden floor or smooth marble.

Stick the images to the page overleaf and write down five words that describe each. Are there any similarities? Do you see any patterns?

# Stimulate with Scent

According to recent studies, the smell receptors in your nose communicate with your amygdala and hippocampus, the brain's storehouses for emotions and memories. Although the German poet Friedrich Schiller apparently found he worked most creatively to the smell of rotting apples, the scents of lemon, orange, mint and rosemary are recognized as the aromatherapy stimulants that could help energize your ideas and increase productivity.

Use scent to stimulate your ideas by holding an orange or lemon in your hands. Feel the texture, shape and weight of the orange, and breathe in the smell. If you don't have a citrus fruit to hand, draw and colour in a picture below and imagine the smells it evokes.

Associate the following words with specific smells – for example, love might smell like cinnamon to you, or you could associate summer with the smell of grass. Try to make as many olfactory connections as you can.

Snow

Rain

Summer

Ocean

Forest

Morning

Danger

Love

Joy

Fear

Money

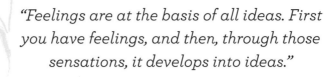

*"Feelings are at the basis of all ideas. First you have feelings, and then, through those sensations, it develops into ideas."*

Jeff Koons, artist

# Emotional Connections

Getting in touch with your deepest emotions, moods and passions can be exceedingly difficult, as we are encouraged by society to control our feelings. This exercise should help you find some cathartic release when emotions are riding high, understand what triggers certain emotions in you, and perhaps channel those strong feelings into a creative endeavour such as painting or story-writing.

Explore your most intense emotions by finishing these sentences.

- ○ I hate it when...
- ○ I get angry when...
- ○ I feel like crying when...
- ○ I am embarrassed by...
- ○ I feel relaxed at...
- ○ I wish he/she/you would...

# Grafitti Tag Your Emotion

Street art and graffiti have long been a form of expressive art to communicate a personal or political message. Use this technique to take a word or image that resonates with how you are feeling right now.

How are you feeling? Write the word over and over in different styles of fonts or tagstyle writing. Harness your inner anarchy and imagine you are shouting the word out to the world.

# Your Favourite Food

Taste is so influenced by smell, sight and the texture of food on the tongue that we often find it difficult to isolate the five sensations: bitter, salty, sweet, sour and the savoury *umami*, so here you will be relying on the memories of a food you love and remember well.

Think about your favourite food. What does it smell like? What attracts you to it? What words can you use to describe the taste? What does it remind you of? Do you associate any memories with this food?

**Take It Further**: Listed opposite are some descriptors used by food writers and wine experts that might help you describe the taste:

| | | |
|---|---|---|
| Acidic | Flat | Refreshing |
| Aged | Fruity | Rich |
| Astringent | Full-bodied | Ripe |
| Bitter | Gamey | Robust |
| Bland | Gelatinous | Rubbery |
| Burnt | Grainy | Sharp |
| Buttery | Grassy | Silky |
| Chalky | Gritty | Slimy |
| Cheesy | Herbal | Smoky |
| Chewy | Hot | Smooth |
| Chocolatey | Icy | Spicy |
| Citrusy | Jammy | Spongy |
| Cloying | Juicy | Syrupy |
| Coarse | Leathery | Tangy |
| Creamy | Lemony | Tart |
| Crisp | Malty | Toasty |
| Crumbly | Mellow | Velvety |
| Crunchy | Minty | Vinegary |
| Doughy | Musty | Watery |
| Dry | Nutty | Woody |
| Earthy | Oaky | Yeasty |
| Eggy | Oily | Zesty |
| Fat | Over-ripe | |
| Fiery | Peppery | |
| Fishy | Pickled | |
| Fizzy | Powdery | |

# CHAPTER 3

## SEE THINGS DIFFERENTLY

New perspectives, reframing and problem solving are the key themes of this chapter, which includes exercises that challenge your automatic responses and viewpoints. Sometimes simply looking at an object with fresh eyes can transform it completely. The aim here is to help you enhance your problem-solving skills and ability to find creative solutions, and to think "outside the box".

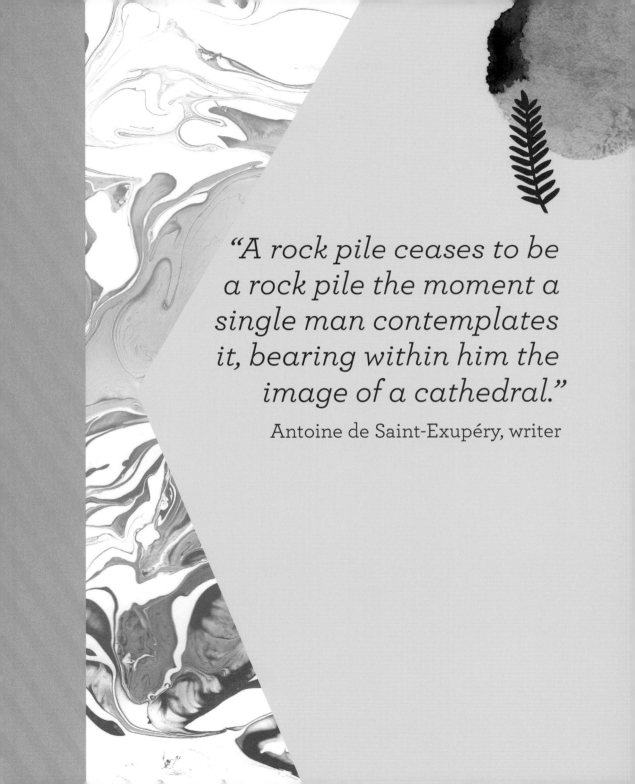

"*A rock pile ceases to be a rock pile the moment a single man contemplates it, bearing within him the image of a cathedral.*"

Antoine de Saint-Exupéry, writer

# Remake A Masterpiece

What if Van Gogh's *The Starry Night* was a moonless night? Or the *Mona Lisa* was crying instead of smiling? Or the couple in Grant Wood's *American Gothic* held guns instead of pitchforks?

In the spirit of the irreverence that created these original masterpieces, take Edvard Munch's *Scream* and make it joyful – or subvert another painting of your choice. Examine the colours and shapes and change them to the positive. Where would you position the hands? Would the figure be alone?

# Create a Wise Counsel

Break the pattern of using the same solutions to problems over and over again by creating an imaginary mentor or "wise counsel" as a resource for advice. Considering how this person would handle an issue will prevent you from falling into your predictable assumptions and thinking habits.

Think about your personal role model and the attributes they have that you admire. It could be an historical figure, a modern-day leader, a family member or teacher, or an amalgam of the best qualities from a range of individuals. Now list their top ten attributes below – you might list good judgement, moral compass, persistence in adversity or artistic ability. Consult your counsel whenever you need a fresh take on a problem.

1 ................................................................................................................................

2 ................................................................................................................................

3 ................................................................................................................................

4 ................................................................................................................................

5 ................................................................................................................................

6 ................................................................................................................................

7 ................................................................................................................................

8 ................................................................................................................................

9 ................................................................................................................................

10 ..............................................................................................................................

## Your Round Table

Perhaps just one person can't embody all the qualities you need, so create a Round Table group of mentors. It's like having your own personal government making decisions that are in your best interests.

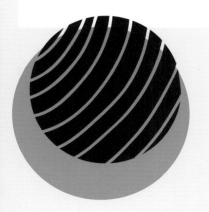

# Imagine Your Avatar

This is a displacement exercise in which you transport yourself into another environment. It's really helpful in reframing any specific issues or questions you're wrestling with, but it also allows you to stand outside your own skin and see yourself from a more objective point of view.

Picture yourself in another country, speaking another language and living a different life, or imagine yourself as an alien in another world altogether. Would your reactions and decisions be different from what they are now?

○ What do you look like?

○ How do you dress?

○ What do you eat?

○ Where do you live?

○ How do you communicate, or what language do you speak?

○ What is your job?

○ Do you have a family?

○ What is your physical environment like?

**Take It Further**: Imagine yourself as a superhero or warrior, someone much more powerful than you are. What skills and talents do you have? How would this superhero version of yourself handle your problem?

# In Five Years, In Ten, In Twenty

Human beings tend to look at the short term – what's affecting you right now or what's coming up in the next six months. Imagining how your life and the world might look in the future can not only help you get a better perspective of what's important in life but also enable you to appreciate "the now".

Take a moment to close your eyes and imagine what your life would look like 5 years from now, 10 years from now, 20 years from now.

○ What does it look like if you stay on the same path you are on, and how does that make you feel?

○ What would you like to see yourself doing in 5 years? In 10?

○ Where do you see yourself in 20 years' time? Does the thought make you feel happy, excited or content?

# Find the Silver Lining

Everyone has a rain-cloud day, but if your own personal storm cloud seems to be following you around, try answering these five simple questions. They may help you to find the silver lining.

On the left-hand page overleaf, draw your rain cloud and label it with your problem. Make it as stormy and dark as you feel. Add in some lightning bolts or raindrops.

On the right-hand side, draw your sunny blue sky with fluffy white clouds. You are now going to find your silver lining. Ask yourself these questions and add them to the picture:

1 What can I learn from this?

2 How can this positively affect me?

3 How will this help me on my life's journey?

4 What idea or opportunity does this give me?

5 How does this make me stronger?

# Six Thinking Hats

Sometimes you just need to begin again with a blank slate. If you're struggling with an idea or can't find a solution, break it down by looking at it from different perspectives. Using a system designed by the father of lateral thinking, Edward de Bono, put on a different-coloured hat and ask yourself these six questions:

1 **Blue hat**  What is the idea or problem and the goal? Look at the big picture.

2 **White hat**  What are the actual facts?

3 **Red hat**  What's your gut feeling? How do you feel about it? What emotions do you associate with it?

4 **Black hat**  What could go wrong? What are the issues?

5 **Yellow hat**  What could go right? What's the best possible outcome?

6 **Green hat**  What's the alternative, or where else could this idea or problem go?

*"Logic will get you from A to B.
Imagination will take you everywhere."*

Albert Einstein, physicist

# Cut-Out Collaging

Juxtapositioning is a powerful artistic tool, allowing you to make new associations of images or words. The artist Salvador Dalí was a master of this, placing objects in unusual settings, such as his *Lobster Telephone* or his melting pocket watches in *The Persistence of Memory*.

Cut out a variety of images, slogans and random words from magazines, newspapers and advertisements, and stick them on these pages. You might like to experiment with wacky colour combinations, combine different shapes, or reassign slogans or words to unrelated images to make surprising new connections.

# Mind Map

A mind map is a diagram that connects information around a central subject, and it can be used to unleash your brain's creativity by grouping concepts by association. It can help you generate ideas, find deeper meaning in a subject, and identify any gaps in your thinking.

You can do a mind map for any creative problem you're trying to solve or any action you want to take. Try filling out the sample below to get started. Use words, images, numbers and colours in your mind map as it's been proven that the more mediums you use, the easier the information is to remember, and more connections can be made.

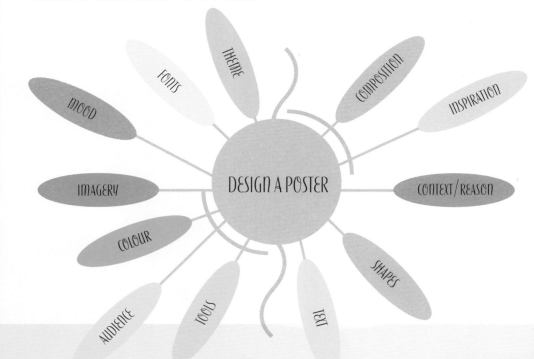

# Mind-Map Poster

Now that you've done all the background thinking and planning, you can make your mind map into a real poster.

Draw it here freehand using coloured pencils or pens. Your inspiration could be movie, travel, vintage or propaganda posters.

# My Grateful List

Negative thinking can really derail your mood and your productivity, whereas a positive mental attitude helps your brain to think more creatively. Thinking positively also enhances your problem-solving abilities.

Write down 10 things you are grateful for today. Even if it's as simple as "I got out of bed and went to work" or "That salad I had for lunch was tasty", if it makes you feel "not negative", it counts as making you feel good!

1 ............................................................................................................

2 ............................................................................................................

3 ............................................................................................................

4 ............................................................................................................

5 ............................................................................................................

6 ............................................................................................................

7 ............................................................................................................

8 ............................................................................................................

9 ............................................................................................................

10 ..........................................................................................................

# My Favourite Things About Me

Building up positivitiy and self-esteem will help make you mentally robust, able to tackle anything life throws at you, and give you the optimism to communicate your ideas clearly and effectively.

Write down 10 things you like about yourself. They can range from "I have good hair" or "I'm physically strong" to "I'm a hard worker" or "I'm always there for my friends and family".  Think about the following categories: physical attributes, cognitive skills, talents, emotional wellbeing, personality.

1 ........................................................................................................................

2 ........................................................................................................................

3 ........................................................................................................................

4 ........................................................................................................................

5 ........................................................................................................................

6 ........................................................................................................................

7 ........................................................................................................................

8 ........................................................................................................................

9 ........................................................................................................................

10 ......................................................................................................................

# CHAPTER 4

## PLAY WITH WORDS

This section features games and activities to help you make new linguistic connections and experiment with language. Whether you've hit a creative-writing block, have an essay looming and no ideas, or just want to have fun with words, these activities will help bolster your cognitive abilities, memory and mental health.

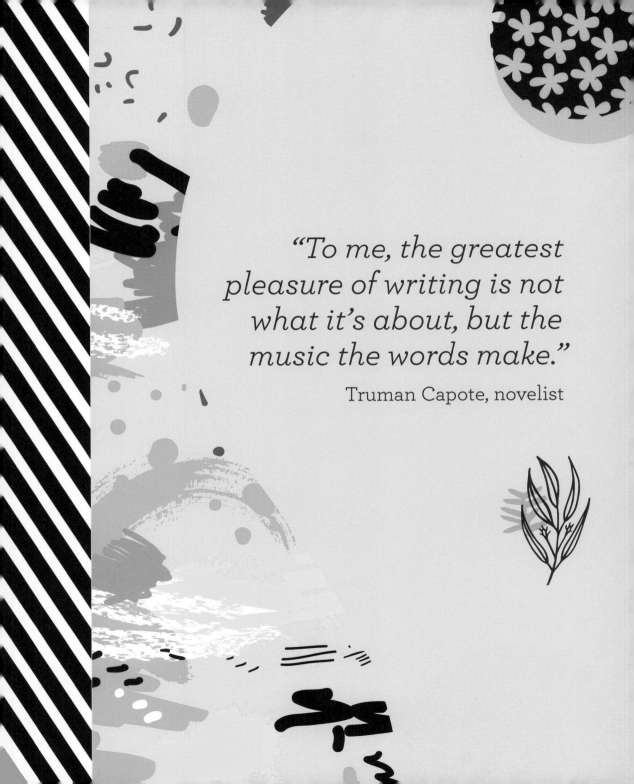

"To me, the greatest pleasure of writing is not what it's about, but the music the words make."

Truman Capote, novelist

# Mirror Writing

The artist and inventor Leonardo da Vinci wrote most of his personal notes in mirror writing, and mirror-writing calligraphy was popular in the Ottoman Empire during the eighteenth and nineteenth centuries. Changing the physical movements to perform a task will help stimulate your creativity and engage the right side of your brain.

- ○ Write your signature as you normally would below – left to right.

- ○ Now write your signature in reverse as mirror writing – starting from the right and working left.

- ○ Now write your name upside down, then on an angle.

# Word Association

Playing this word-association game will let your imagination run freely and get creative ideas flowing. It helps make new connections in the brain.

Write a trigger word below, such as "bird" or "ocean". Under it, write the next word that pops into your head, then immediately write down the next word that you think of. Don't think too much about it, just keep writing and making associations. When you're finished, look at the words and see if you can find any patterns or trends.

**Take It Further:** Write the trigger word in the centre of a page and draw a circle around it, now mind map the associated words – connecting the circled words with lines or arrows radiating outwards so that each new word becomes a new trigger word.

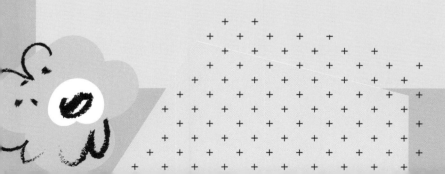

# Pictogram Writing

Long before emojis, pictograms were symbols used to represent a concept, object, activity, place or event, and formed the basis of such systems as cuneiform writing and hieroglyphics. Today they are all around us: from the skull and crossbones used to denote poison to traffic signs and app icons. Accustoming your brain to pictorial writing will expand your ability to communicate in a non-verbal form.

Draw symbols and pictures instead of writing words to form sentences. Use connecting words to make the sentences complete if you need to, but try to include as many symbols as you can.

# New Lyrics to Your Favourite Song

Songwriters are inspired by many sources, not simply their own emotions or experiences. They could be influenced by a news story, an overheard conversation or something they've seen. Here you will use clues such as these to create your own song.

Listen to a favourite song. Now make up your own new lyrics to the music. To get started, first think of a new title for your song, or at least the general theme. Be guided by the music itself: is it a ballad, dance music, angry or mournful?  Write your lyrics on the page opposite.

# Bowie Poetry

The singer-songwriter David Bowie famously used a technique of cutting out unrelated words and sentence fragments, and rearranging them to create his lyrics. He claimed the unconscious intelligence that came from the pairings of ideas was a powerful tool for his compositions.

Cut out words and sentence fragments from newspapers, your own writings, books, flyers or advertisements. Rearrange them, ransom-note style, on the pages opposite and overleaf to create lines of poetry. When you are happy with the results, stick them in place.

*"Poetry is a deal of joy and pain
and wonder, with a dash of
the dictionary."*

Kahlil Gibran, philosopher

# Freewriting for a Minute

This technique is often used by writers struggling with a block, and it can help free up ideas and rid you of anxiety and stress.

Set your timer for one minute and write anything that pops into your head – a complete stream of consciousness. It doesn't need to make sense, or be grammatically correct or spelled or punctuated correctly. Keep moving your hand across the page all the time and don't stop.

Then set your timer for five minutes and write continuously. Work your way up to an hour of stream-of-consciousness writing.

# He Said, She Said

Good dialogue can move a plot forward, create a situation of conflict, reveal a character's personality or motivation and show the nature of the relationship between characters, but can also be used outside creative writing to expand your perspectives and reactions to situations. Try this dialogue-writing technique to open your mind to alternative ideas. Also listen to conversations that you can hear around you – on the street, in shops or on public transport.

Take these following starter dialogues and create the responses – think about gender or context and consider how those might change the reaction. After each response, add in emotional clues for the characters, such as "(frightened)" or "(accusatory)".

Sam: "What did you think I was going to do?"

_____

"The city looks so beautiful at night," whispered Kat.

_____

Charlie: "What's wrong with him? Do you know CPR?"

_____

"Then I realized you had lied to me," said Eleanor, "and I wondered for how long."

_____

# Random Words

Designer and researcher Balder Onarheim has noted that the ability to make random associations with words is an important part of being creative. A good example of this happening in the world of music is hip-hop artists who free-associate random rhyming words when improvising.

Write down the first words you think of next to those below as quickly as possible. If it helps you to make it into a rap sentence, then do that too.

Earth _Heaven_

Campfire _Song_

Toothbrush _Paste_

Violin _Viola_

Rainforest _Monkey_

Ballet _Shoes_

Padlock _Key_

Beard _Mustache_

Cathedral _Church_

Lightning _Zap_

Salt _Pepper_

Cup _Pint_

Yacht _Boat_

Feather _Bird_

Cement _Stairs_

# Dream Journalling

Studies have shown that creative performance increases for people who have been prodded to reflect on their dreams, and that people who recall more dreams tend to score higher on creativity tasks.

Keep this book by your bedside and when you wake up, immediately jot down your dreams. If you can't remember them don't worry, just keep a daily record, as there will be days when you can recall your dreams and days when you can't. Take note of the environment, the feeling, the action and context. Describe the characters that inhabit your dreams and any recurring motifs, and rate the details and vividness.

# CHAPTER 5

## EXPLORE THE VISUAL

Finding expression in drawing, design and painting is the focus of this chapter; here you will be able to experiment with different art techniques, working with colour, line, texture and form. Some of the ideas explored in the pages that follow originate from art-therapy techniques, and will help you to holistically connect the visual and physical world with the intuitive and emotional.

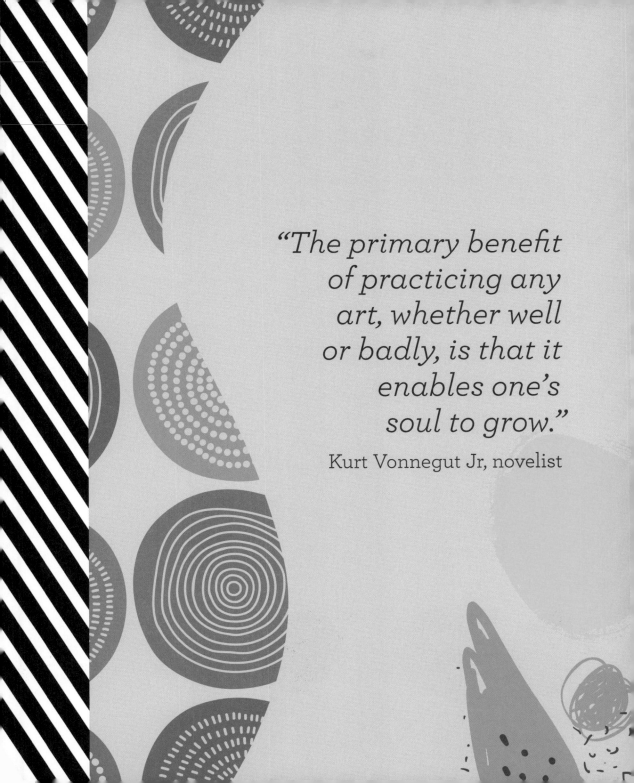

"The primary benefit of practicing any art, whether well or badly, is that it enables one's soul to grow."

Kurt Vonnegut Jr, novelist

# Leaf Repeat Patterns

Decorative patterns use the repetition of lines, shapes, tones, colours and shapes to explore the possibilities of a simple shape. Here you will copy the outline of a leaf and see how many repeat patterns you can create by arranging the copies in various configurations.

Draw a template of a leaf. It can be any type, such as oak, maple, birch, and a stylized design or natural sketch. Just make it simple enough that you can cut out 12 identical shapes from plain paper.

Now experiment with arranging the leaves in different patterns. Organize them them into columns or rows, offset them like bricks, arrange them randomly, or centre them with all the stems pointing inward. See how many types of patterns you can create.

When you achieve a pattern you like, trace around the templates on a sheet of paper and colour them in, adding details and markings. You may like to make them all the same or give each a different colourway.

*"For an Impressionist to paint from nature is not to paint the subject but to realize sensations."*

Paul Cézanne, artist

# Continuous Line Drawing

This technique is achieved by drawing a single unbroken continuous line, without lifting the pen or pencil from the paper, to render an image. With practice, it will help you to closely observe the lines of the subject, its contours, shadows and overall shape.

Choose a subject. It can be a coffee cup on your desk, a clock on the wall. Start with a clean, simple shape: you can always progress to more complicated forms later. Using a pen, marker, or graphite pencil, start at one point and draw without lifting the pen, tracing around the shape, drawing in details and going back on the line if necessary.

# Negative Space

A beginner's drawing technique, this involves shading in the space around a subject (the negative space), rather than the subject itself.

Take a subject from real life or a photograph or digital image, such as a tree. Sketch in the negative space, leaving the subject as the white paper. If you're struggling with this, use coloured pencils, chalks or markers to shade in the negative area.

# Make Your Mark

Mastering mark-making techniques can enhance your drawing and painting skills and enable you to add texture and pattern to your work. The marks can be precise and tidy, or loose and gestural.

Using a pen or pencil, try out the techniques below. Vary thick or thin lines and light or heavy pressure to get different results.

- **Gradiant shading** Using a pencil to increase the greyscale from white to dark; helps develop your shading control.

- **Stippling** Small dots, made close together or spaced out; useful for creating shading and light and dark areas.

- **Dashes** Short lines, made in various directions; useful for rendering fur and fabric.

- **Crosshatching** Drawing parallel lines close together, then repeating another layer on top of the first in the opposite direction, thus creating a "linen" effect.

- **Scribbling** Small random squiggles; great for creating foliage effects.

Gradient shading

Broken lines

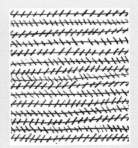

Shells

Herringbone

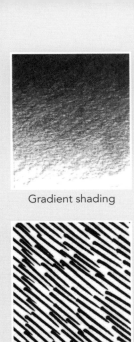

Diagonal lines

Lines, dots and dashes

Lines and spirals

Crosshatching

Squiggles

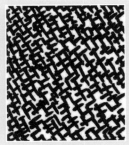

Dashes

Parquet

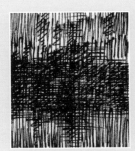

Dense hatching

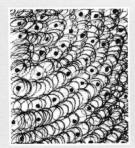

Dots and scribble

Stippling

Loops and dots

A bit of everything

*"Art enables us to find ourselves and lose ourselves at the same time."*

Thomas Merton, Trappist monk

# Non-Dominant-Hand Drawing

This is a great way to loosen up your drawing and make new connections between brain and hand. It will encourage you to let go of control and judgement, and embrace a more fluid and child-like method. It's often used in art classes as a warm-up to help enhance the integration of the two sides of the brain.

Place your drawing instrument in your non-dominant hand and either draw from a subject, such as a photograph or a real object, or simply doodle and draw a collection of abstract images.

# Changing Hues

It is always interesting to experiment with unpredictable colour palettes to change the mood or atmosphere of a scene.

Find a photograph of a natural landscape – it could be a forest, beach, field or mountain scene, but make sure it shows land, sky and horizon.

Using a pencil, copy the photograph, tracing the main lines. Now, using coloured pencils, colour in the drawing but change the hues completely. For example, you could substitute a bright orange for blue sky, or choose violet for grass, or pink for the sun. How does the colour change make you feel? Is the landscape now more sombre or threatening? Is it more joyful? Do you feel nauseated, claustrophic, free?

# Your Ugly Colour

Do you feel unsettled in a yellow room? Does the colour red stimulate you? Artists and psychologists have long believed that colour can impact people in dramatically different and surprising ways. This exercise will test your emotional response to colour.

Draw a picture of something you love below, but use a colour – or several colours – that you hate.

# Abstract Colour Blocks

Many artists have used blocks of colour to create their art and connect with emotions, from Henri Matisse and Sonia Delaunay to Wassily Kandinsky and Mark Rothko. Here you will be making abstract colour blocks to explore the arrangements of colour and shape.

Choose your subject. It could be the food on your plate, the person sitting opposite you on a train, a view outside your window. Look at it in terms of blocks and shapes of colour only. Colour in what you see using paints, markers or pencils: don't draw in details, just wash in blocks of colours, almost as if you were near-sighted.

# Meditative Painting

This method will help you to reconnect your mind and body, enabling you to relax deeply while creating. There is no subject to draw or paint or consider. You can use coloured pens, pencils, crayons, pastels, or break out the paints and experiment with acrylics or watercolours.

Arrange all the colours in front of you. Which ones are you intuitively drawn to? Now start to apply colour to the page in squiggles, splatters, broad sweeping strokes or whatever moves you. Don't think: just feel and express, creating lines, shapes and textures instinctively.

*"I never paint dreams or nightmares.
I paint my own reality."*

Frida Kahlo, artist

Draw something from your reality: an event from your past, an object you use every day, a family member, friend or pet you love.

# CHAPTER 6

## MAKE AND DO

This chapter relates to the physical three-dimensional world and how we interact with it – not only our behaviours and actions, but also the objects we use and make. Spending time engaged in crafts and hobbies – from woodworking to knitting – is proven to stimulate the creative centres of the brain, and the activities on the following pages will help to nurture a more fulfilling and rewarding downtime for you.

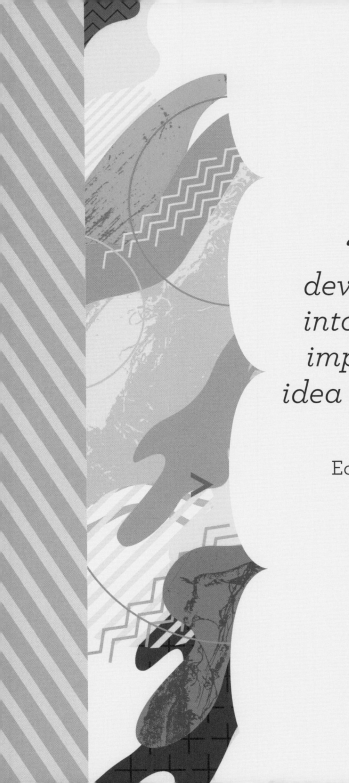

*"An idea that is developed and put into action is more important than an idea that exists only as an idea."*

Edward de Bono, father of lateral thinking

# Do It Backwards

You may find that you've slipped into predictable routines, always rising at the same time, brushing your teeth, showering and having breakfast in exactly the same order, day in and day out. These automatic habits can be stifling your creativity, so try making some changes.

As you go about your day, think how you can interrupt and reverse your daily habits. Try these challenges to shake things up.

- ○ Sleep on a different side of the bed or get out of the bed on the opposite side in the morning.

- ○ Brush your teeth or hair with your opposite hand.

- ○ Have dinner for breakfast, or breakfast for dinner.

- ○ If you always take showers, take a bath instead.

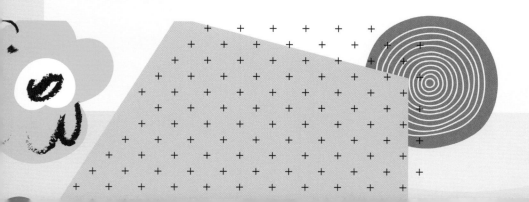

# Reroute Your Journey

Whether you walk, drive, cycle or take public transport, your journey to work, college or school every day can be, at the best of times, rather uninspiring. By simply rerouting your journey, it is surprisingly easy to reclaim this time of the day as your special zone of creativity.

Using the ideas below, change something about your journey each day.

○ Take another route entirely, such as drive through a park on the way to work or take the back roads instead of the motorway.

○ Get off or get on a stop early, or park further away. Walk the remaining distance, taking time to notice new sights, people, the weather.

○ Find another mode of transport. Cycle if you drive; take a bus instead of the train.

○ Sit in another part of the train or bus; queue in a different place.

○ Share a ride – pick up colleagues or friends and make time for conversation with them.

○ Keep a travel journal and draw or write down all the sights you see throughout your journey, including landmarks, architecture, signs, advertisements and people.

# Twenty Circles

Based on an exercise developed by Stanford professor Robert McKim, this idea focuses on the act of doing, rather than the quality of the end result. By engaging fully in a timed activity like this, you circumvent your thought processes; you won't be able to consider whether the idea is good or bad, you just have to be engaged with it!

Set a timer for two minutes, then start filling in all the circles below as fast as you can. You might have an overall theme, such as faces or patterns, or completely random designs.

*"Creativity is thinking up new things.*
*Innovation is doing new things."*

Theodore Levitt, economist

# Build Your Dream House

Designing your dream home can unleash your imagination and enhance your spatial understanding. It can also make you think about how to build – the materials you need, the site, the overall design style and the natural resources you might have available for your build.

Draw your dream home here. Before you begin, consider where it is located. If it's in a city, is it a high-rise? If it's near water, is it on stilts? Is it on a hill? Maybe it's a treehouse! What material is it made from?

   Now consider the configuration of the rooms. What rooms are on each floor? Where are the windows? Is there a garden? You may want to draw both an exterior view and a floorplan blueprint.

# Open Doors

This is an exercise to make you think about the interface between the interior and the exterior, and if what we see on the outside bears any resemblance or gives us clues as to what we might find within. In other words, should we judge a book by its cover?

Make the rectangles below into doors, drawing in details such as door knockers, windows, the door frame and the house number. Think about what each door is used for and the world it opens up into. Is it a door to a home, a barn, a church, a prison? Is the door a portal to another world?

# Reinvent an Invention

Here you will take an established invention and transmogrify it – switching it up and making it perform better or differently.

Consider the individual items below and try to imagine them differently. Now list their new attributes. For example, in a fantasy world, would binoculars see in x-ray or 3D?

**Vacuum cleaner**     **Kettle**     **Hairdryer**     **Screwdriver**     **Bicycle**

# Do an Impossible Thing

Don't be limited by your preconditioned thinking! Who says there's a limit to what's possible? Maybe you just haven't thought of a way of doing it yet.

Make a list of five things that you think are impossible to do, and then imagine how you could do them.

1

2

3

4

5

*"To invent, you need a good imagination and a pile of junk."*

Thomas Edison, inventor